The Lizard Peninsula

Paul White

Bossiney Books

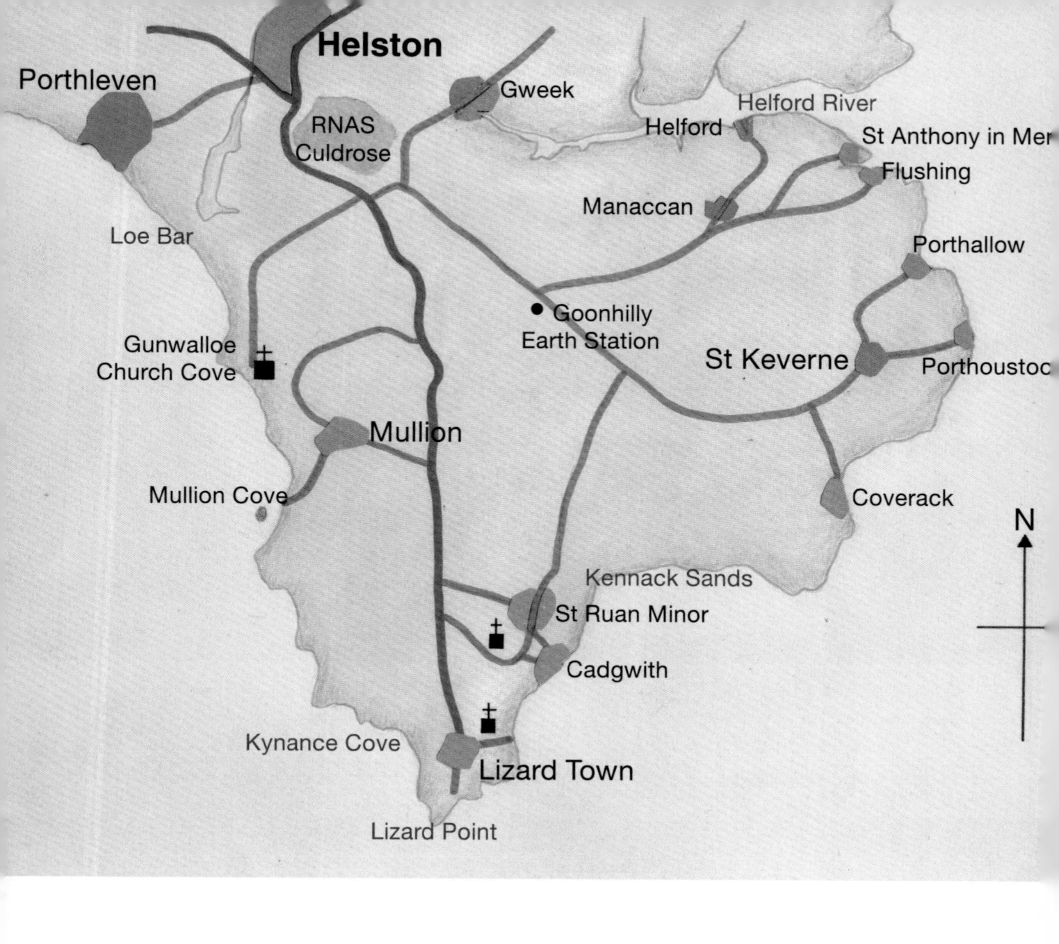

This second edition first published 2017 by
Bossiney Books Ltd, 33 Queens Drive, Ilkley, LS29 9QW
First published 2002

ISBN 978-1-906474-60-7

Acknowledgements

The map is by Graham Hallowell. Colour photographs by the author, except that on page 32 which is by Fred White.
The photograph on page 13 by kind permission of the RIC Photographic Collection.

Printed by R Booth Ltd, Penryn Cornwall

Introduction

The Lizard peninsula is a very special place and in many ways different from the rest of Cornwall. For a start it is almost cut off by the Helford River and by the smaller River Cober, which flows from Helston down to Loe Pool, so it is a peninsula sprouting from a peninsula. It has always been relatively remote, and this is its main attraction to holiday-makers today – except for those who just want to stand at the most southerly point of Britain.

Apart from fishing and farming, the only industry has been quarrying the many and varied rocks, some of them of no particular value except as roadstone, but some of great interest even to non-geologists, such as serpentine, which is not found elsewhere in Britain and which occurs on the Lizard in many different colours. This beautiful rock is locally worked into ornamental pieces, and the amount quarried is now strictly limited. The story of how serpentine came to exist here and here alone is extraordinary and fascinating (see page 15).

Serpentine-based soils are not particularly fertile and most common plants will not grow in them, but certain rare species depend on large

Cottages at Coverack

amounts of calcium or magnesium which they find in serpentine and in gabbro, which is also found locally. The result is that the Lizard can boast of many plants which are found nowhere else in Britain, and rare insects which feed only on these plants. So for anyone with an interest in geology, botany or entomology the Lizard is a paradise, but they will need more specialist books than this one, which is intended as a general introduction to places which I have enjoyed visiting over the last fifty years.

The way to enjoy the Lizard is to stop rushing about, to walk the coast paths and appreciate being where you are, rather than thinking of the next place to go to. Unfortunately the large central car park of Lizard Town (as the village is known) is not the most attractive of places, and there always seem to be visitors parked there entirely at a loss as to why they have bothered to come – which is a great shame: there is in fact much to do.

For a selection of circular walks, mostly along the coast path with an inland return route, please see my book *Shortish Walks on and around The Lizard* (Bossiney Books). Personally I always like to have with me the excellent Ordnance Survey 1:25,000 map (Explorer 103). But every part of the coast path is attractive, and returning the same way along the cliffs is never boring, so don't let the lack of a map or walks book deter you.

Even if you are not able to walk very far, you will find the atmosphere of the Lizard eminently relaxing, particularly if you explore the eastern area of the peninsula – once known as Meneage and not then regarded as part of 'the Lizard' proper. Here there are delightful unspoilt villages, accessible by car, neglected by most tourists and ideal for a leisurely stroll and a cream tea or a pub lunch.

The eastern side of the Lizard is relatively sheltered from the awesome Atlantic gales which attack the western coast; trees can grow here, so the landscape is altogether gentler than in the west – although it is sometimes noted that they do not grow quite as elsewhere, and in particular that Autumn does not make as much of a show as in inland areas.

But east and west alike will astonish you with their wild flowers for much of the year, and a visit between April and June will be a revelation.

Paul White

The south

Landewednack Church

Lizard Town is an unplanned sprawling village which expanded to serve the Victorian tourist industry, providing accommodation and refreshment and numerous workshop/showrooms for local craftsmen making objects from serpentine, as it still does today. (Ironically Lizard Town itself actually lies south of the serpentine area.)

If you turn left (east) in the square (past Ann's Pasty Shop, which can be recommended to all pasty connoisseurs) and bear right at an ancient stone cross, you will come to the parish church, surrounded by trees. It is an attractive building, the tower being patterned with serpentine and granite. The parish is called Landewednack, and the church is dedicated to St Winwallo, whose real name probably began with a 'G' and survives in Brittany as St Guénolé, and on the Lizard as Gunwalloe.

For Cornish people this church has a special poignancy: the 18th century antiquarian William Borlase wrote that:

> After the restoration [1660] we find the Cornish language surviving only in the more western parts, where the

The coast north of Church Cove

> Rev. Mr F Robinson, Rector of Landewednack, is the last that I have met with who, not long before the year 1678, preached a sermon in the Cornish language only.

In the nineteenth century, the rector of neighbouring Ruan Minor claimed the ancient right of sending a horse into a certain field in Landewednack at harvest time and taking away as many sheaves as the horse could carry. This probably reflects an earlier time in which there was just the one parish of St Rumon, which was later divided into four smaller parishes.

Church Cove

The car park in the middle of Lizard Town ('the Green') is the centre-point of a number of radiating walks to the sea, which is about 1 km to the east and the same to the south or to the west. It is therefore possible to walk east past the church and down to Church Cove, then follow the coast path round to the south and back until you are due west of the village, and return to the car park – a walk of about 6.5 km in all, with some fabulous views – or to cut short your walk at any point and return more directly to the village.

There is no legitimate parking beyond the church, so leave your car there, or in the centre of the village if you are planning the circular walk. The oldest and certainly the most picturesque cottages in the parish lie between the church and the sea, including one of three storeys, which is most unusual for Cornwall: this is said to have been at one time an ale-house serving the local fishermen. Church Cove was the original settlement centre.

The lifeboat station

Walk south from Church Cove and you soon arrive at the lifeboat station in Kilcobben Cove. This station was opened in 1961 to replace two previous stations, that at Cadgwith which had been operating since 1867 and saved 388 lives, and the older Lizard station in Polpeor Cove, which had operated since 1859 and saved 562 lives. There was a further lifeboat station at Porthoustock. In the early days, all used rowing boats.

Coastal wild flowers

Wherever you walk along the coast path on the Lizard you will find, especially in Spring and early Summer, the most amazing arrays of

wild flowers, some of them extremely rare, as they grow only on serpentine. Special management techniques, including cattle grazing the cliffs, are used to maintain them.

You will need a better than average book of wild flowers to identify such wonders as Ciliate rupturewort and Prostrate dyer's greenweed, not to mention the Green-winged orchid and the Spotted cat's ear dandelion, but even a botanical ignoramus such as myself cannot but enjoy the great variety of colour.

One of the more noticeable flowers on the cliffs is shown below: the Hottentot fig (*Mesembryanthemum edule*), though much appreciated by visitors, is a vigorous exotic escaped from gardens and so regarded as an invasive weed by conservation experts, rather as is the rhododendron elsewhere in Cornwall.

Lloyds signal station

The waters around the Lizard are still hazardous, but in the days of sail the number of vessels wrecked here was very great indeed. It was possible for a ship to be swept helplessly by unexpected winds or currents, or, in those days long before radar or GPS systems, to drive headlong onto the rocks in dense fog.

The Lloyds signal station, shown above, was partly responsible for some of the wrecks. Sailing vessels coming from Australia or South America had been out of telegraphic contact with their owners for many months, so a system was established whereby they reported on arrival to the signal station, using flags. The signal station would send a telegram to the owners, who then replied with an instruction for the master to sail for a particular port, and that signal was relayed by flags to the ship.

The effect of this system was to keep vessels hovering around these highly dangerous waters.

The *Queen Margaret* was a four-masted ship, one of the fastest sailing vessels ever built, which in 1913 was kept waiting too long for her instructions (perhaps the owners were having a long lunch) and drifted onto rocks just offshore from the old lifeboat station. She was a total loss but all the crew survived.

Marconi's experiments at the Lizard

It is strange to think that in 1900 most scientists believed that radio signals could not be transmitted unless transmitter and receiver were within sight of each other.

Guglielmo Marconi, the great pioneer of radio, set up a station in these wooden huts at Housel Cove as an all-weather ship-to-shore communication centre, but he also used them to communicate with another station on the Isle of Wight, 300 km distant. This was achieved in January 1901 – a great increase on the 7 km which was the record distance only three years earlier, which comprehensively proved that radio had a great practical future. The huts have been restored by The National Trust to their original plan: the larger provided the living quarters, the smaller housed the equipment. The station operated until 1913.

Marconi's much more substantial station at Poldhu (see page 28) was also completed in 1901, and was to be responsible for even greater advances, communicating with Newfoundland late that year, and with Australia by 1924.

The lighthouse and the Lion's Den

The first light at the Lizard was erected by Sir John Killigrew in 1619, and was a private venture. The government in those days was delighted to allow someone to pay for the right to provide a light and collect 'light dues' from shipowners who had passed it. There was much local opposition, as stripping wrecks was seen as a necessary part of the local economy; moreover there were some who thought Sir John's own vessels – which were mostly devoted to piracy – would gain an unfair advantage. In the event Sir John's agents couldn't get the shipowners to pay up and the light was soon abandoned.

The next light was established by Trinity House in 1752, with the twin towers still to be seen. Each then had a coal fire in a brazier on the roof! Coal was replaced by oil in 1812 and by electricity in 1878.

At the same time a foghorn was installed, but shipwrecks in fog continued despite it. The light became automatic in 1998 and nowadays is controlled from Harwich. The lighthouse is open to visitors on most days in the summer.

Another feature visible in the photograph, at the top of the cliffs to the left of the lighthouse, is the Lion's Den. This massive chasm was formed when a cave collapsed on 19 February 1847. Surprisingly the lighthouse keeper reported he had heard no sound when this happened, according to CA Johns whose book *A Week at the Lizard*, first published in 1848, is still a fascinating read. Such catastrophic collapses are part of the otherwise slow process by which the coast is eroded. In time the original arch of the cave will also collapse, making the chasm into a cove. Another fine example is the 'Devil's Frying Pan' just south of Cadgwith.

Housel Cove, where the photograph opposite was taken, is home to the Housel Bay Hotel, opened in 1894. It was fashionable with royalty and high society and also with artists and writers in the years before the first world war. Tourism in Cornwall at that time was the prerogative of the rich, although already a genteel lady was complaining that 'The Lizard is full of trippers of a very second rate description.' Such 'trippers' would certainly not have been working class people, since reaching Cornwall was well beyond most people's pockets, even if they could take time off.

A bus service from Helston Station was established in 1903, and the attraction of standing at 'Britain's most southerly point' must have been all the greater in those days when only the richest could afford foreign travel.

Kynance Cove

The artists and writers who flocked to Housel Bay Hotel came not least because of the fame of Kynance Cove, which the Victorians appreciated as one of the most beautiful places in Britain, long before the railways made Cornwall accessible.

Murray's guidebook of 1859 describes it in painterly terms:

> The rocks appear as if they had been purposely grouped; and by their dark but varied colours pleasingly contrast with the light tints of the sandy beach and azure sea. The predominant colour of the serpentine is an olive green, but this is diversified by waving lines of red and purple, while many of the rocks are encrusted by the yellow lichen, or warmed by veins of steatite. The fragments into which the cliffs have been dissevered are pierced by caverns which are beautifully polished by the waves, and the beach is strewed by gorgeous pebbles…

And it is indeed a most remarkable and magically beautiful place, which never fails to surprise and delight.

The rocks and caves all have imaginative names – Lion Rock, Goat Rock, Toad Rock, Parlour Cave and the Drawing Room, Asparagus Island (on which wild asparagus grows) and the Devil's Bellows and Letterbox which, if you are there at the right stage of the tide on a day with a good swell, provide entertainment with a water spout and a suction draught sufficient to take a sheet of paper from your hand. But take care.

The geology of the Lizard peninsula

The rocks of the Lizard were once apparently quite separate from the rest of Cornwall. They were formed (most unusually) in the 'Moho', the area within the earth between the 'mantle' and the 'crust', and were squeezed out in a thin slice some 380 million years ago. The Lizard rocks collided with 'Euramerica' (Europe + North America) a mere 300 million years or so ago, and were pushed northward by the other super-continent of 'Gondwana' (Africa + South America), which then waltzed onwards leaving the Lizard like a smudge of the other chap's paintwork after a glancing car crash.

The junction of the Lizard rocks and Cornwall is a fault-line which runs in a curve across the peninsula from Polurrian Cove, where it can be seen, to Porthallow.

There are several types of serpentine, two of which occur at Kynance. All were formed under enormous heat and pressure from peridotite, the material of the earth's mantle. Most of Kynance Cove is formed of tremolite serpentine, which apart from being fine grained and many coloured has the property of absorbing heat from the sun – so be careful if you touch it.

If you become interested in the local geology, you should obtain a copy of *Beneath the skin of the Lizard* (Cornwall Council), an excellent booklet which suggests geological walks and is well illustrated with colour photographs and diagrams.

Soapy Cove

The beautiful walk along the cliffs to the north of Kynance Cove brings you to Gew Graze, or Soapy Cove, so named after the soap-rock or steatite, a light coloured soft stone which was mined here from 1750. It was used to make porcelain before china clay was discovered, and more than 40 tons was extracted each year.

It was never easy to make a living from farming the exposed headlands with their poor serpentine soil; part-time work quarrying for steatite or serpentine probably kept many families solvent, along with a little fishing or smuggling. The fashion for polished serpentine ornaments began in the 1830s, especially after 1846 when Prince Albert purchased one. The main quarry was at Poltesco, north of Cadgwith, where the Lizard Serpentine Company operated from 1838 to about 1893. The remains of the works can still be seen on the beach there.

Lizard Point, with the old lifeboat station

Cottage in Lizard Town

Lizard Town

The growth of the tourist industry in the 1890s led to an increase in the number of buildings in the village, and a shift of emphasis from the church and Church Cove towards the green, where the visitors arrived by bus from the railway station at Helston. As well as catering for the visitors with food and accommodation, the village had by the 1930s acquired some thirty workshops from which craftsmen – almost all of them local men – sold ornaments made on the premises. Many had learned their craft at the old works at Poltesco. A scarcity of suitable stone has reduced the number of craftsmen to a mere half-dozen today.

Cadgwith

This picturesque fishing hamlet just north-east of Lizard Town is justifiably popular with visitors. A dozen or so boats still fish for crabs and lobsters. You need to park in the main car park and walk down the path to the cove. Many of the white-washed cottages are thatched, as most Cornish cottages were (by DIY methods) until slate came into general use in Victorian times. Some of the roofs are chained down against the wind.

Like most fishing coves, Cadgwith probably began life in the middle ages as an uninhabited cluster of fishing 'cellars' on the shoreline. These would have been used by the farmers of the village of Ruan Minor, who fished as a sideline, as a place to store their equipment and in the fishing season to process the catch. Only later, when the population began to increase dramatically in Tudor times, would it have developed into an inhabited hamlet.

The headland from which the photograph above (and many thousands of others each year!) was taken is called the Todden.

The east

Gweek

Now famous for its seal sanctuary, on the north bank of the Helford River, Gweek was probably a port even in pre-Roman times. There are a number of Iron Age earthworks surrounding the port, most notably those at Gear and Caervallack. Whether the Romans themselves had any presence here has not yet been established: three rectangular earthworks remain to be excavated.

For a time the borough of Helston controlled Gweek, which was their port. (It is possible that Helston once was a port itself, before the development of Loe Bar, but this is far from certain.) The borough erected a gallows at the port, to remind potential wrong-doers that they had the legal power to execute criminals.

For centuries the port profited from the rich tin area of Wendron, with ore shipped out and timber, coal and building materials imported up the river but, as with so many other Cornish ports, the silt caused by the mining industry made the channel gradually shallower and the port less economic to use. In the nineteenth century timber for the mines was sometimes brought up the river lashed into rafts.

Today the sheltered muddy creek is home to many yachts and classic working boats.

Manaccan

This attractive inland village lies at the heart of the area called 'Meneage', the 'monkish land', though it is not clear where the monks were based. The church is dedicated to St Manacca, a saint of whom nothing is known, who is also honoured at Lanreath near Polperro. The church is Norman in origin, though rebuilt in the fifteenth century, and has a famous ancient fig tree growing from one of its walls.

Manaccan is still very much a 'real' village, inhabited all year round, and – at the time of writing – still has a popular pub.

Helford

This delightful village, with its numerous thatched cottages nestled among woodland on a creek, is well worth the drive along narrow lanes from Manaccan to reach it. The large car park is discreetly sited a short walk from the centre of the village, which boasts a pub, and

The Norman south door of Manaccan church

also a pedestrian ferry to Helford Passage opposite, which is just a short walk from the beautiful gardens of Glendurgan (National Trust) and Trebah.

Looking at this peaceful little village now, it is hard to believe that it was once a significant port with its own Customs House, as had Gweek. The Helford estuary was a magnificent natural harbour in the days when ships were generally under 200 tons; it would have been developed commercially if the even finer facilities of Falmouth had not been so close – and with better access to the commerce of inland Cornwall. At Helford cargoes could be off-loaded into barges for transport to Gweek.

Trade with the hinterland of Meneage can never have been great, and the suspicion must be that the two Customs Houses and a Preventive vessel based in the river were there to deter smuggling, for which the Helford was ideal: it is the first safe harbour for boats coming from France, and the many quiet creeks make ideal concealed landing places.

It was not only smugglers who valued the Helford for its seclusion. Shakespeare's contemporary Richard Carew wrote:

> Hailford, so called of the fordable river Haill, if elsewhere placed would carry the reputation of a good harbour, but as it now

standeth, Falmouth's overnear neighbourhood lesseneth his use and darkeneth his reputation as quitting it only to the worst sort of seafarers, I mean pirates, whose guilty breasts, with an eye in their backs, look warily how they may go out ere they will venture to enter; and this at fortified Hailford cannot be controlled, in which regard it not unproperly brooketh his more common term of Helford, and the nickname of Stealford.

He probably had in mind the notorious Killigrew family.

Daphne du Maurier no doubt drew on this historical reputation when she wrote her romantic novel *Frenchman's Creek*.

The creek, more correctly known as Frenchman's Pill, is just a short walk from Helford village. From the west side of the village, take the 'Public Byway' which winds up the hill. At the top turn right. Cross a cattle grid, then keep left and follow the signs. There is a beautiful woodland walk beside the Pill, though the water is often tantalisingly obscured by luxuriant vegetation.

St Anthony-in-Meneage

The southern shore of the Helford estuary ends at Dennis Head, where a royalist garrison held out for three years in the Civil War. Cornwall remained staunchly royalist throughout that war and towards its end

Above: The beach at Porthallow
Opposite: St Anthony-in-Meneage church and beach

Cornishmen had hopes that the King would negotiate independence for Cornwall as a royal enclave separate from the Commonwealth of England. This was not to be. In the end Dennis Head was abandoned and so were Pendennis and St Michael's Mount.

South of Dennis Head lie the hamlet and church of St Anthony-in-Meneage, virtually on the beach, overlooking Gillan Creek, which runs parallel to the Helford, up to Manaccan. This is a place of great tranquillity and charm, where you can quietly watch people messing about in boats.

If you are heading for the east coast of the Lizard, a narrow lane leads around the edge of Gillan Creek, or you may prefer the slightly wider road by way of Manaccan.

Porthallow and Porthoustock

Locally pronounced 'Pralla' or 'P'thalla' and 'P'roustock', these two fishing villages are among the least affected by tourism in the whole of Cornwall. Remoteness, together with a major roadstone quarry – abandoned, but always a temptation for developers – which used Porthoustock as a port, have preserved both villages for visitors who appreciate their authenticity and calm.

St Keverne

This large village actually feels more like a small town: it serves the whole of the eastern Lizard, and its large church beside a substantial square suggests its ancient importance.

The churchyard contains many graves of shipwreck victims. The unforgiving rocks of the Manacles reef offshore have claimed hundreds of vessels and more than a thousand lives, 106 of them in a single night in 1898 when the liner *Mohegan* took a suicidal course straight into the reef.

There are good cliff walks south of St Keverne; many walkers circle inland to take in Tregellast Barton, home of Roskilly's farm, famous for its ice cream and other produce.

For Cornish people St Keverne has a symbolic significance as the home of Michael Joseph an Gof, one of the leaders of the uprising of 1497, when a Cornish army marched on London in protest against paying taxes to support a war against Scotland, and were defeated at Blackheath. An Gof was executed but claimed that he would have a 'memory immortal' and he is indeed remembered with respect today. This statue shows An Gof and his fellow leader, the lawyer and MP Thomas Flamank

Coverack

This fishing village is another of the delights of the eastern Lizard, a sheltered spot with a miniature harbour wall.

The Paris hotel is named after the liner *Paris*, which with 756 people aboard ran ashore on Lowland Point in 1899, only eight months after the loss of the *Mohegan* on the Manacles. This time the passengers and crew were all rescued, and the liner was refloated a few weeks later – only to strike the Cornish coast again, and be refloated again, later in her career!

Just south of Coverack lies an attractive row of cottages called Sunny Corner: admiring some early vegetables in a garden, I was told there is a micro-climate here. Rain-clouds pass straight over the narrow heights of the Lizard and deposit their load when they next hit high ground. And certainly there is good shelter from sou'westerlies.

Beyond the cottages you come to the strangely reptilian shape of Chynalls Point, and the cliff path may well tempt you further.

Inland

The peninsula forms a plateau; its central area is remarkably flat and rather featureless, except for the huge dishes of the Goonhilly Earth Station, which was able to handle more than half a million international phone, fax and computer calls at the same time, so continuing the telecommunications tradition of Marconi. It included a very successful visitor centre. With the changes in technology brought about by mobile phones and the internet, Goonhilly was closed by BT in 2008, with the visitor centre closing two years later. The site has now reopened as Goonhilly Earth Station, controlling various satellites and carrying business internet data.

RNAS Culdrose, a large airbase specialising in helicopters, has a public viewing area. Its operations include helicopter training, anti-submarine warfare and air-sea rescue.

The Lizard's heathland, though often rather featureless to look at, contains some unique plants which grow only on serpentine

Helston

The town has for centuries served as the urban centre for the Lizard, even though it lies at the very edge of the peninsula.

Helston is of very ancient origin: its old name was Hen-lis, meaning 'old court'. In 1201 it acquired a charter as a borough, and was already involved with the mining industry, later becoming a 'coinage town', where ingots of tin had a corner (*coin* in Norman French) removed for assay and taxation purposes – hence Coinagehall Street.

An interesting town trail leaflet is available from the Tourist Information Centre, and there is an excellent museum in the former Butter Market.

The famous Flora Day or 'Furry' is held every 8 May (unless that date is a Sunday or Monday) when there is dancing in the streets throughout the day to the catchy tune of the Flora Dance, not to mention a mummer's play and other festivities. The event is thought to be of pre-Christian origin.

At the foot of Coinagehall Street stands the Grylls Memorial, which the Rev Sabine Baring-Gould scathingly described as 'designed for execution in sugar-candy, and carried out in granite'

The west

Loe Bar

The Bar is a sandbank which blocks the Cober River, creating a fresh-water lake behind it, Loe Pool. There are walks along either bank of the lake. The bar looks like a wonderful beach, and so it is if you want to walk or sun-bathe, but on no account should you swim here. There is a steep slope just underwater which creates fierce currents and an undertow.

The beach deceived the captain of HMS *Anson*, who in 1807, finding his vessel in distress in a storm, tried to beach her on the apparently gentle slope – only to strike the equivalent of a cliff just a short distance from safety. The masts fell; some of the crew scrambled to safety, many were drowned. A local man, Henry Trengrouse, was in the crowd which watched in horror, unable to get a rope to the ship. He spent the rest of his life inventing and perfecting a rocket apparatus for use in such circumstances.

Gunwalloe

A little further south you will find Gunwalloe Church Cove, a favourite place for many families. The church is protected from the sea by an outcrop of rock, but for centuries there have been fears for its safety. The tower is separate from the nave, and may be the remains of an older church.

A small cove between Church Cove and Jangye-ryn is called 'Dollar Cove', because a Spanish ship wrecked there in the 1780s was supposed to be carrying 2 1/2 tons of dollars, some of which washed ashore.

Poldhu

An attractive short walk along the cliffs from Gunwalloe, or a circuitous drive inland, brings you to Poldhu Cove (see photograph on page 31). This is dominated by a former hotel, now a care home, which was built in 1899 for the tourists who were brought by the new railway to Helston.

Shortly afterwards, Marconi built his radio station here, from which the first transatlantic radio communication was achieved, on 12 December 1901, and the first with Australia in 1924. The station continued in use until 1934.

Above: Loe Bar, and the memorial to the loss of HMS Anson

Below: By contrast with Loe Bar, the beach at Gunwalloe Church Cove is ideal for paddling, and sometimes for swimming when lifeguards are present, with sand of good quality for sandcastle-building

Mullion

The village of Mullion is the main population centre on the west side of the Lizard. Its people seem to have preferred the sea to farming. Fishing was always important, and the Rev. E G Harvey, who wrote a book about his parish in 1875, tells us that 'men living may even now... be heard to speak proudly of the day when they were engaged in the smuggling service'.

Smuggling was a major industry in which all levels of society, even including the squire and the clergyman, not to mention the magistrates, colluded against the government.

In 1916 RNAS Mullion – the predecessor of RNAS Culdrose – was built as an airship station to find and destroy U-boats, with two huge hangars near Bonython manor.

Mullion Cove

Mullion Island forms a natural breakwater to the south-west of the Porth Mellin, as the cove used to be called. There was a successful pilchard fishery here in early Victorian times, but later in the century the pilchards deserted the coast – none at all being taken from 1859-64, and few thereafter. The two piers of the present harbour were not started till 1893, when Lord Robartes hoped to encourage both the fishery and other trade, perhaps including tourists arriving by boat.

A lifeboat was based here from 1867-1909. Between January 1867 and March 1873 there were no fewer than nine wrecks immediately in the area of the cove, costing 69 lives, whilst the lifeboat saved just three lives in its entire career.

Above: Poldhu Cove

Below: Looking down towards Mullion Cove

Some useful contact details

Helston Tourist Information Centre (01326) 558881
www.visithelston.com

Cornish Seal Sanctuary, Gweek (01326) 221361
www.sealsanctuary.co.uk

Flambards Theme Park (01326) 564093 www.flambards.co.uk

Goonhilly Earth Station www.goonhilly.org

Helston Museum (01326) 564027 www.helstonmuseum.co.uk

Lizard Lighthouse (01326) 290202

Marconi Centre, Poldhu (01326 241656)
www.marconi-centre-poldhu.org.uk

National Trust Lizard Countryside Office (01326) 561407
www.nationltrust.org.uk/lizard-point

A Bossiney walks book

Shortish Walks on and around The Lizard (5-9 km walks)